A Mirror Image

by David Bauer

STECK-VAUGHN
A Harcourt Company

www.steck-vaughn.com

Look at the pattern on the moth.

What do you see?

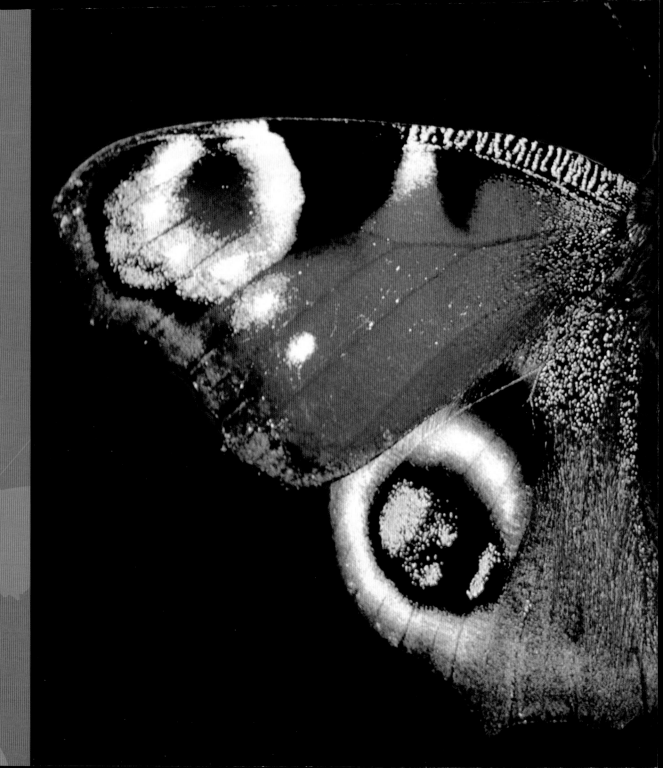

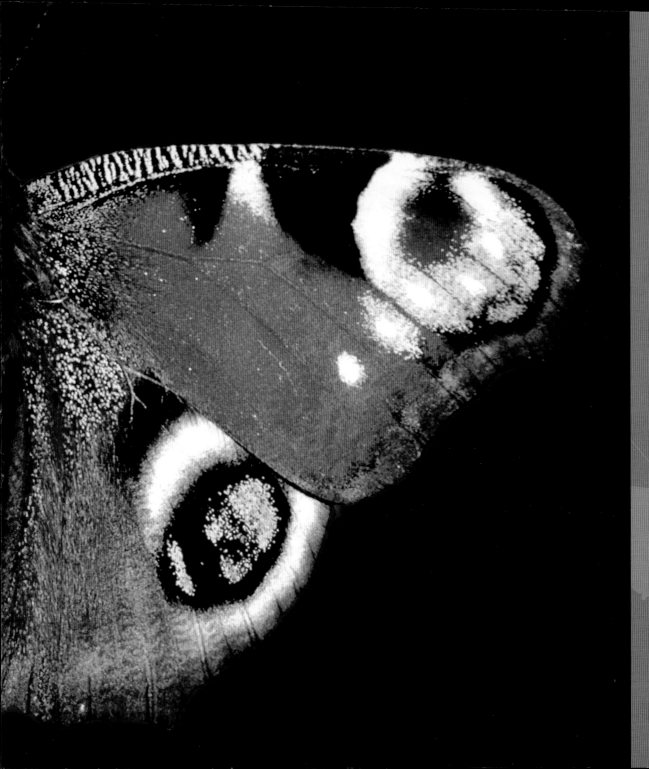

The pattern
on one side
is a mirror
image of
the pattern
on the other
side.

Look at the shape of the snowflake.

What do you see?

4

The shape on one side is a mirror image of the shape on the other side.

Look at the patterns on the turtle.

What do you see?

The patterns on one side are a mirror image of the patterns on the other side.

Look at the face of the monkey.

What do you see?

The face on one side is a mirror image of the face on the other side.

Look at the shape of the dragonfly.

What do you see?

10

The shape on one side is a mirror image of the shape on the other side.

Look at the face of the cat.

What do you see?

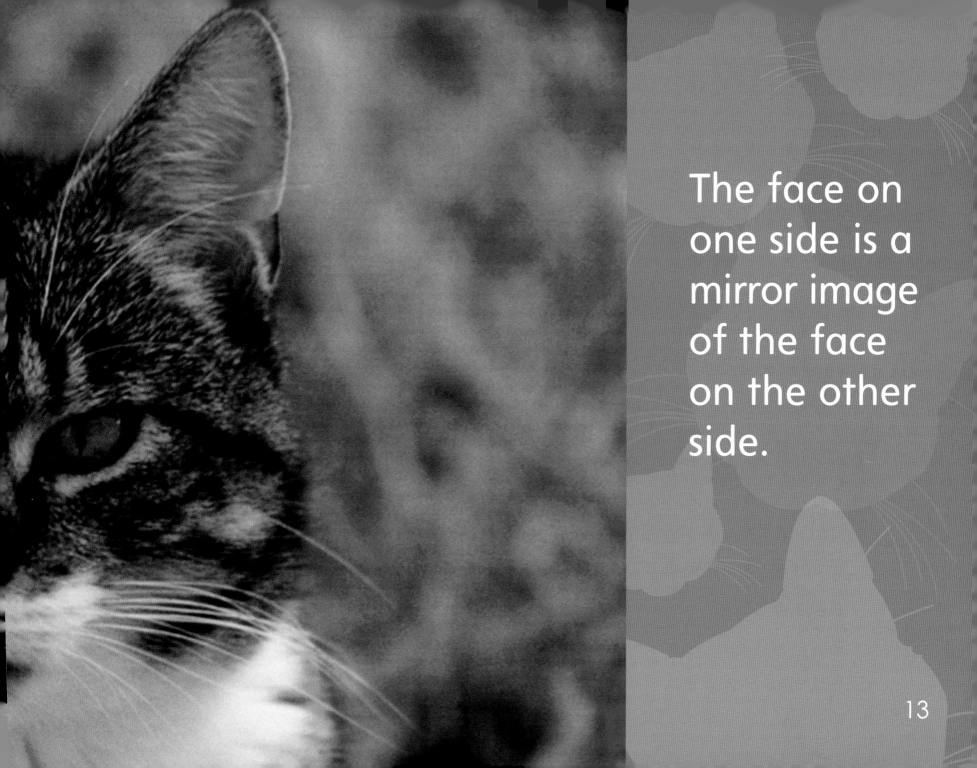

The face on one side is a mirror image of the face on the other side.

13

Look at the shape of the owl.

What do you see?

The shape on one side is a mirror image of the shape on the other side.

Show how each picture has a mirror image.

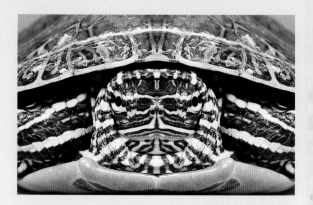